GREATEST MOVIE MONSTERS™

WEREWOLVES

DANIEL E. HARMON

rosen publishing's
rosen
central

Published in 2016 by The Rosen Publishing Group, Inc.
29 East 21st Street, New York, NY 10010

Library of Congress Cataloging-in-Publication Data

Harmon, Daniel E., author.
Werewolves/Daniel E. Harmon.—First edition.
    pages cm.—(Greatest movie monsters)
Includes bibliographical references and index.
Includes filmography.
ISBN 978-1-4994-3521-4 (library bound) — ISBN 978-1-4994-3523-8 (pbk.) — ISBN 978-1-4994-3524-5 (6-pack)
1. Werewolves in motion pictures—History—Juvenile literature. 2. Werewolves—Folklore—Juvenile literature. I. Title.
PN1995.9.W38H37 2016
791.43'67—dc23

                                                                        2014045479

Manufactured in the United States of America

On the cover: Benicio del Toro portrays Lawrence Talbot (the werewolf) in *The Wolfman* (2010). The movie won an Academy Award for Best Achievement in Makeup for Rick Baker and Dave Elsey's artistry.

CONTENTS

CHAPTER 1

WEREWOLVES THROUGH HISTORY

Panic gripped southwestern France in 1603. Children were vanishing, never to be seen again. A baby was taken from a cradle inside a family cottage. A girl tending cattle on a farm was attacked by a large, wolflike, sharp-fanged beast. She managed to drive it away with a prodding tool.

A teenage boy admitted to the acts, claiming he was a werewolf. He said he'd met a man in the forest who had given him a wolf skin to put around himself. The boy bragged of killing and devouring the children.

Authorities decided he was insane. They ordered that he be confined in a monastery. He died there eight years later. It was said he had fingernails like claws and long, pointed teeth.

At about the same time, an even more savage episode occurred in Germany. Town leaders found Peter Stubbe (or Peter Stumpf) guilty of being a werewolf. For more than twenty years, he was said to have killed and eaten men, women, children, and cattle. Victims included his own daughter and sister.

Stubbe's punishment: He was tortured and beheaded. His body was burned to remove all trace of him.

Farm folk of the Le Gévaudan province of France in the 1760s claimed a werewolf killed hundreds of people. They described a wolflike monster that walked upright and emitted a dreadful stench. After three years of terror, a posse tracked and shot the creature. Exactly what they killed is a mystery. Most believe he was not a werewolf but simply a gigantic, man-eating wolf.

THE LIFE AND DEATH OF PETER STUMP

Sixteenth-century sketches depict the horrible record of Peter Stubbe (also recorded as "Stump" and similar spellings). He was executed for allegedly slaying and devouring humans and livestock.

Suggestions of werewolves go back more than two thousand years. Ancient Greek historians described them as mythological figures. Some myths told of humans being cursed by gods to lives as werewolves. According to other lore, people might become werewolves after being infected by the bite of a werewolf.

Warriors of ancient armies disguised themselves in wolf skins for the purposes of spying and surprise attacks. This practice possibly contributed to people's ideas about werewolves.

Rumors of werewolves became rampant in Arcadia. In this rural, mountainous region of Greece, wild animals abounded. Wolves were a particular menace to livestock.

The image of werewolves as monsters reached its height in European countries during the late Middle Ages. Superstitious people grasped for explanations to violent mysteries they could not explain. Sometimes, they accused neighbors and even relatives of being werewolves.

Early accounts held that the devil gave werewolves their power and set them upon their communities. Most of the descriptions are similar. Peter Stubbe in werewolf form was said to resemble a gigantic, powerful wolf. He had lethal claws and a wide mouth revealing sharp teeth. His wild, penetrating eyes shone like fire in the dark.

A WEIRD ASSORTMENT OF SHAPE-SHIFTERS

A werewolf, in mythology and folklore, is a type of shape-shifter. A shape-shifter is said to be a creature that magically, mentally, or medically can change from one animal form to another. This change may be a shift from a human to a furry, feathered, or fish creature—and vice versa. It can also suggest a change from one human being to another. Shape-shifters, old and new, have become extremely popular in modern fantasy fiction.

The werewolf is one of many legendary shape-shifters. Fearful people all over the world have believed in terrifying, half-human creatures throughout history. A vampire, for example, is a fictional shape-shifter that ordinarily appears as a likeable

Shape-shifting characters are found in centuries-old literature of many world cultures. This image from Norse folklore shows Loki, a clever human who could change appearances, at a supernatural feast.

THE MANY WORDS FOR "WEREWOLF"

The ancient Greeks called werewolves lycanthropes. The word was a combination of their terms for "wolf" and "man." In the earliest references, it did not describe men who changed into wolves. Rather, it described men with wolflike traits—hairiness or savage appetites.

"Lycanthrope" is the word scholars frequently use today when discussing werewolf creatures. The ability (or imagined ability) to change between a human and wolf is called lycanthropy.

In different parts of medieval Europe, various forms of the word "werewolf" were mentioned. "Were," or "wer," referred to adult men. Different spellings included "werwulf," "wariwulf," and "weriuwolf."

In some South American countries, a wolf man is called Lobizon.

human. By night, though, the individual attacks other humans. It drinks their blood to become immortal. The vampire takes on the blood-sucking traits of bats. Some vampire characters have batlike wings.

In Irish and Scottish folklore, selkies live in the ocean as seals. When they come ashore, they become humans. In ancient Norse literature, Loki was a wily being who interacted with gods. Loki could change forms and even switch genders.

Swan maidens and dove girls are found in the mythology of various peoples. They are females who transform from humans to birds.

By the 1700s, serious belief in werewolves and other shape-shifters had faded in most countries. For the most part, they had become subjects of scary stories.

CAUSES, CURES, AND DEFENSES

Many causes of becoming a werewolf have been suggested. They include these:

- A curse by an ancient god, devil, or sorcerer
- A bite or scratch by an existing werewolf
- Sleeping outdoors beneath a full moon on a particular calendar date
- Drinking a secret mixture of herbs and liquids (a variety of ingredients have been mentioned)
- Drinking water from a magical lake or stream
- Drinking muddy water from an animal's paw print

People living in Europe during the late Middle Ages believed a werewolf could be cured. Numerous remedies were considered. The simplest treatment was to strike the creature on the head with a knife. Another idea was to hunt it down until it became exhausted.

Herbs with medicinal powers have been suggested. Wolfsbane, a poisonous flower, has often been included in the plots of horror films, books, and stories. Wolfsbane, also called monkshood, was said to be a cure—or at least a temporary antidote—

Monkshood, an intriguing class of flower that includes wolfsbane, is poisonous. However, in small doses it can be a pain reliever. In fiction, it is considered an antidote to lycanthropy.

to both vampirism and werewolfism.

Wolfsbane is very dangerous. In times past, warriors rubbed the flower on their arrow tips. They also put wolfsbane in enemy water sources. However, in small, careful doses, it has been prescribed to relieve pain and restore health. Some historians believe wolfsbane potions might have been used as mind-distorting drugs. Drugs today can make people have weird dreams and delusions. In the same way, wolfsbane may have caused individuals to think they could become animals.

In the first major werewolf movie, *Werewolf of London* (1935), a rare Tibetan plant, mariphasa, was believed to provide an antidote. Mariphasa (which does not exist) was said to be a light-sensitive flower. Curiously, it bloomed only in moonlight, not sunlight. This trait seemed linked to the belief that werewolves were active only during the full moon phase.

In most werewolf literature, death has been the only real solution to the individual's condition. As for defenses, potential victims allegedly could be protected by wolfsbane. Some believed special prayers or magic spells could also drive away werewolves.

FROM RED RIDING HOOD TO SIDESHOWS

Little Red Riding Hood is a fairy tale character famous in many countries. A big bad wolf stalks her while she is walking through woods to her grandmother's house carrying a basket of goodies. The wolf slyly takes the elderly woman's place beneath the bedcovers, concealing its evil head with a nightcap. It waits to pounce on the grandchild.

The story was first published in 1697. It no doubt had been handed down for centuries before then through word of mouth. Originally, it had a terrible ending: the wolf ate Red Riding Hood and her grandmother. Happily, today people read the version of it that was published in *Grimm's Fairy Tales* (1812). The Brothers Grimm introduced a woodsman who comes to their rescue.

Some historians suspect there is a connection between this fable and werewolf lore. They think it is rooted in medieval tales of witches who wore red hoods and danced in a forest with werewolves and vampires.

Writers have told of strange bonds between humans and wolves throughout much of recorded history. Romulus and Remus, for example, were twin sons of the god Mars in Roman mythology. As infants, according to the myth, they were cast into a river to die. But they got ashore and were raised by a she-wolf. Mowgli, the Indian boy in Rudyard Kipling's *The Jungle Book*, was a feral (wild) child raised by wolves.

Stories of "wild men" covered with hair and living in the woods like animals have been told for centuries. Some are at least partly true. In the 1700s, an Englishman named John Biggs became disgusted by society and went to live alone in a cave. An Oregon newspaper article in 1885 reported the frightful case of John Mackentire. He had disappeared while hunting in the mountains. Four years later, other hunters came upon a figure resembling Mackentire—except he "had grown hairy as an animal, and was a complete wild man." The man they saw was eating a deer carcass. He ran away when they approached.

Long before movies, entertainment promoters made money off people's fascination with "wild men" and "wolf men." Sideshows at carnivals and county fairs have exhibited scary, hair-covered people. Sometimes they were caged or rattled iron chains to frighten customers.

In most sideshows, the performers' makeup, wigs, and fur wraps were obvious. Some, though, genuinely were quite hairy. A medical condition called hypertrichosis, or "werewolf syndrome," causes extreme hair growth. In some cases, hair grows all over the body.

Fedor Jeftichew (1868–1904) had a friendly but hair-covered face. P. T. Barnum, the illustrious showman, exhibited him as "Jo-Jo the Dog-Faced Boy." Julia Pastrana (1834–1860) had long hair growing from her face and limbs. Her promoter Theodore Lent, who married her, billed her as the "Bear Woman."

The fascination people have with werewolves is understandable because they are such horrifying creatures. Most people, though, accept that actual werewolves never existed.

Julia Pastrana had a medical condition that resulted in extraordinary facial hair growth. She was one of several hairy individuals displayed as sideshow attractions during the 1800s.

CHAPTER 2

HAIRY CREATURES TAKE TO THE SCREEN

In 1913, Universal Studios (then known as the Universal Film Manufacturing Company) released an eighteen-minute silent film titled *The Werewolf*. It was based on an 1898 short story about Native Canadian wolf-humans (*loups-garous*) who terrorized white settlers.

The Werewolf is believed to be the first movie to draw from werewolf lore. Over the next four decades, it was followed by other motion pictures on the subject. Most of the early films are hardly known except to film historians. They took various approaches to lycanthropy and its causes. For example, in a 1924 movie titled *The Wolf Man*, the central character turned beastly as a result of excessive drinking.

Most notable among the early werewolf movies was *Werewolf of London* (1935). It cast the wolf creature in an unusual plot. It opened with English scientists in Tibet seeking a rare flower that created artificial moonlight. One of them, played by Henry Hull, was attacked and bitten by a wolf/human creature. Not until returning to London did he realize the bite had made him a werewolf. The rare flower sample he had brought back to examine in his laboratory proved to be a temporary antidote. It was not enough to cure him.

When the moon was full, the scientist changed into a werewolf. He committed two murders. On the third occasion, he was killed by police while trying to slay his wife.

Werewolf of London was only a mediocre box office success. The main

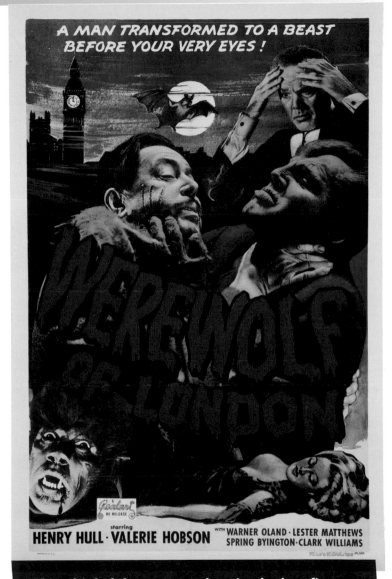

A MAN TRANSFORMED TO A BEAST BEFORE YOUR VERY EYES !

WEREWOLF OF LONDON

starring
HENRY HULL · VALERIE HOBSON   WITH WARNER OLAND · LESTER MATTHEWS
SPRING BYINGTON · CLARK WILLIAMS

This frightful poster advertised the first Werewolf of London movie, made in 1935, which received significant critical attention. The film was not very profitable and did not earn lasting fame.

MAKEUP MAKES THE (WOLF) MAN

It takes time—typically hours—for makeup artists to transform an actor into a convincingly frightful apparition. *Werewolf of London* is little remembered, critics surmise, because lead actor Henry Hull wouldn't tolerate the lengthy prep time needed to depict a memorable monster. His werewolf character appeared more human than wolf.

Jack Pierce was one of Hollywood's best makeup artists. He had created the unforgettable leading character portrayed by Boris Karloff in *Frankenstein* (1931). He had rebuilt Karloff's head into another monster icon the following year for *The Mummy*. But Hull, historians suggest, lacked Karloff's patience in the makeup chair. As a result, his appearance was only partly wolflike.

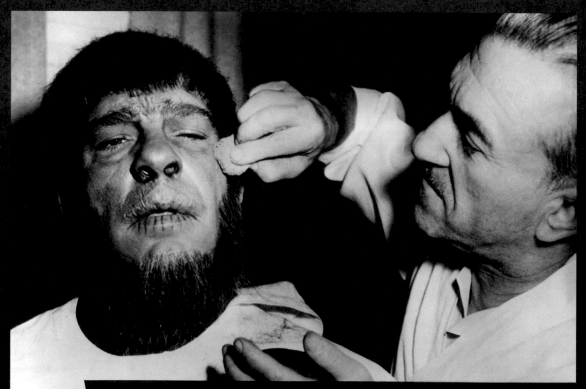

Renowned makeup artist Jack Pierce worked long hours to transform actor Lon Chaney Jr. into his famous monster likeness in **The Wolf Man,** *made in 1941.*

Pierce was hired to "monsterize" Lon Chaney Jr. for the 1941 film *The Wolf Man*. This time, he had greater liberty to create an effective horror creature. The role made Chaney one of Hollywood's most acclaimed monster actors of all time.

A modern-day makeup artist noted for his supernatural creations is Rick Baker. Baker has won numerous awards, including one for the 2010 film *The Wolfman*. He has expressed deep respect for Pierce, whose artistry greatly influenced him. Among his many honors is the 2009 Jack Pierce Lifetime Achievement Award at the Chiller-Eyegore Awards Ceremony.

As a child, Baker was inspired by *The Wolf Man* and *Frankenstein* to learn the art of makeup. As a teen, he experimented with creating artificial human features. He began his career at the age of twenty-two as a special effects assistant in filming *The Exorcist*. He won his first Academy Award for his makeup work in *An American Werewolf in London* (1981). He was also instrumental in the production of the music video *Michael Jackson's Thriller* (1983).

reason, film historians believe, was that Hull's character was not sufficiently hairy to be scary.

Then came the film that brought to the screen a horribly believable lycanthrope. It would send chills down the spines of generations of moviegoers.

A HOLLYWOOD MONSTER CLASSIC

Larry Talbot, an Englishman in his thirties, has not seen his father for eighteen years. When his older brother dies in a hunting accident, he returns from America to the family estate in Wales and begins to repair the strained family relationship. But instead of healing, he soon finds himself caught up in an entangled, deadly foray into the supernatural.

So begins the classic 1941 horror film *The Wolf Man*, released by Universal Studios. It's the movie in which the werewolf attains epic monster status on a par with the Frankenstein monster.

Soon after his return, Larry (played by Lon Chaney Jr.) is experimenting with a telescope that was given to his father, Sir John Talbot (Claude Rains). Looking through it into the village, he's attracted to Gwen Conliffe (Evelyn Ankers), a beautiful young woman working in her father's antique shop. Smitten, he visits the shop to meet her. While there, he buys a cane adorned with a silver wolf's head and pentagram figure. Gwen explains, to Larry's amusement, that it symbolizes a werewolf. She recites a rhyme (which is repeated periodically in the film):

> *Even a man who is pure in heart and says his prayers by night*
> *May become a wolf when the wolfbane blooms and the autumn moon is bright.*

That night, Larry goes with Gwen and her friend Jenny to a gypsy fair. Outside the encampment, Jenny is attacked by a gypsy man-turned-wolf named Bela. Larry rushes to help. Although too late to save her, he kills the creature with his cane—but not before being bitten.

Larry is suspected of murdering Bela the human. He explains to the village constable that his encounter was with a wolf, not a man. For proof, he attempts to point out the bite mark, but the wound has healed miraculously. Returning to the camp, he meets a gypsy woman named Maleva. She tells him that Bela, the slain werewolf, was her son. Because Larry was bitten, she says, he has also become a werewolf.

Maleva, a strange gypsy woman, reveals the werewolf curse to Larry Talbot, doomed as a result of being bitten by her son. The scene is from the 1941 classic **The Wolf Man.**

Larry is still not convinced—but is no longer amused—by the talk of werewolves. He must face the reality of his curse, however. Taking on a wolflike transformation, he sets forth at night and kills a grave digger. Finding wolf tracks at the death site, authorities decide to set animal traps in the woods.

The next morning, Larry awakens in his room, changed back to a human. To his shock, he sees the paw prints of a wolf on the floor beside his bed.

In his next transformation, Larry is caught in one of the wolf traps. Before he is captured, the gypsy Maleva finds him and sets him free.

Larry and Gwen are falling in love. Realizing the threat he poses, he tells her that he must go away forever, without her. He then confides to Sir John what has happened to him. His father dismisses his story as a delusion. At his son's insistence, though, he leaves Larry tied in a chair before going to join the hunters stalking the killer wolf. Larry persuades him to carry along the wolf-headed cane.

The film ends in foggy woods at night, where Gwen has gone to search for Larry. He has returned to wolf form and broken free of his bonds. In his uncontrollable passion for blood, he attacks the woman he loves. Sir John runs to her aid and slays the creature with Larry's strange walking cane. The corpse returns to human form. When the constable and hunters arrive at the scene, they conclude that Larry died while saving Gwen from the wolf.

SPECIAL EFFECTS, THEN AND NOW

The making of *The Wolf Man* was a formidable test of patience and endurance for Lon Chaney Jr., the actor who portrayed the werewolf. The audience saw his transformation from a human to a hairy, ferocious wolf in just a few moments onscreen. What they didn't know was that those fleeting seconds took hours for the production crew to capture on film.

Technicians marked the exact position on the set where Chaney, initially as a human, appeared in front of the camera. Chaney then went to makeup artist Jack Pierce for the first application of wolf's hair (which actually was the hair of an Asian yak). Then it was back to the set, where he repositioned himself for the beginning moment of the transformation. This process was repeated many times, with a heavier layer of makeup applied each time. Gradually, the film crew obtained a sequence of shots that, when compiled, showed Chaney as Larry Talbot transformed into Chaney as the Wolf Man.

Special effects today are created largely with computer technology. For the 2010 film *The Wolfman*, the werewolf makeup for actor Benicio del Toro required only three hours to apply. Makeup artist Rick Baker reported that although he won an Oscar for his work in the film, much of what viewers saw onscreen was digitized.

THE IMPACT OF *THE WOLF MAN*

The Wolf Man did not receive major film awards, although it was nominated for several American Film Institute lists. However, it has had a lasting impact not just on movie making but on other entertainment media. It was also an important achievement in the careers of several of its principals.

Lon Chaney Jr., the title character, portrayed werewolves in numerous films during the next twenty years. Most notable were *Frankenstein Meets the Wolf Man* in 1943, *House of Frankenstein* in 1944, *House of Dracula* in 1945, and the comedy *Abbott and Costello Meet Frankenstein* in 1948. His final wolf appearance was in a Mexican movie, *La Casa del Terror* (*House of Terror*), in 1960. Scenes from that movie and

Writer/director Curt Siodmak (right), shown here on the set of the 1958 House of Frankenstein *movie, was the mastermind behind the successful 1941 werewolf film.*

a previous Mexican film about mummies and robots were assembled four years later in *Face of the Screaming Werewolf*. Chaney's role was that of a werewolf mummy.

Because of *The Wolf Man*, Chaney became best-known for his monster roles. He starred in three 1940s films as the Mummy. But he often referred to Hollywood's Wolf Man as "my baby." He died in 1971.

Curt Siodmak, a science fiction novelist and screenwriter, scripted *The Wolf Man*. He had been successful as a writer in Europe before immigrating to the United States in 1937. But it was his creation of Hollywood's version of the werewolf legend that brought him fame. Drawing from witch and vampire lore, Siodmak introduced the notion that a werewolf could be slain only by a weapon made of silver. He also penned the movie's somber poem: "Even a man who is pure in heart . . . may become a wolf when the wolfbane blooms. . . ." The verse was used in later werewolf films.

Siodmak went on to write scores of novels, stories, and screenplays. Among his movie scripts were two more films that involved the Wolf Man and starred Chaney: *Frankenstein Meets the Wolf Man* and *House of Frankenstein*. Siodmak's autobiography, published in 2001 (the year after his death), is titled *Wolf Man's Maker*.

The Wolf Man is also the best-known work of its producer/director, George Waggner.

CHAPTER 3

RAVING ABOUT WEREWOLVES

Hollywood filmmakers took notice of the popularity of the 1941 monster classic. They immediately followed up with the lycanthrope theme. Spine-chilling growls and howls of werewolves became common cinema fare in the 1940s.

A year after *The Wolf Man* came out, *The Mad Monster* appeared on theater screens. The United States recently had entered World War II, so, not surprisingly, the movie plot had a military connection. In the film, an American scientist believes he can make soldiers stronger by injecting them with wolf blood. Other scientists mock his theory. In an experiment, he succeeds in creating a monstrous wolf-man—and turns it against his critics.

Since then, werewolf movies have spun a variety of plots. Settings range from teen hangouts to city streets. Here are notable examples.

- *Frankenstein Meets the Wolf Man* (1943) is the first in a string of movies that feature two or more popular film monsters.

The Wolf Man, Larry Talbot (again played by Lon Chaney Jr.), comes back to life when grave robbers open his crypt to steal valuables. In the process, they remove the vital wolfsbane that had been placed in his coffin to prevent his revival.

- *Cry of the Werewolf* (1944) stars Nina Foch as a gypsy who changes to wolf form to guard the secret grave of her mother, who also was a lycanthrope. This movie is believed to be the first film since the 1913 silent film *The Werewolf* to feature a wolf-woman.

- A hot-tempered high school student is the main character in *I Was a Teenage Werewolf* (1957). After a series of violent outbursts, the teen seeks help from a psychologist. But the doctor, wanting a test patient for a series of sinister experiments, injects him with a serum that turns him into a werewolf. Michael Landon plays the lead role.

The box office success of the movie prompted the hasty production of two films along similar lines. *I Was a Teenage Frankenstein* and *Blood of Dracula* were written and filmed in one month. They were released later in 1957—in time for Halloween.

- The 1962 movie *Lycanthropus* is also called *Werewolf in a Girls' Dormitory*. The killer werewolf is a teacher at a girls' reform school.

- The public naturally doubts reports of fantastic or supernatural occurrences. Not surprisingly, disbelief abounds in many werewolf movie plots. In *The Boy Who Cried Werewolf* (1973), a teenager (played by Kerwin Mathews) and his father

Actor Michael Landon, who later became a popular star of television westerns, played the lead role in I Was a Teenage Werewolf, *released in 1957.*

encounter a killer wolf while staying at a mountain cabin. The father fights and kills the wolf. Only the son sees the body of the slain wolf change back to the form of a man. Authorities dismiss his story, assuming the dead man is an anonymous tramp. The father, bitten in the struggle, becomes a werewolf. He ultimately passes the curse on to his son—whose story most people continue to disbelieve until the very end.

• Some films give lycanthropy a lighthearted treatment. One of the best examples, *An American Werewolf in London* (1981), is comically fantastic. Two young Americans (portrayed by David Naughton and Griffin Dunne), while backpacking on the English moors, are attacked by a werewolf. One of them dies. He begins to appear to his friend, who is treated at a hospital in London, in visions and dreams. The surviving friend becomes a were-wolf and goes on a murderous spree.

An American Werewolf in London has become a cult classic. A sequel, *An American Werewolf in Paris*, was released in 1997.

Actor David Naughton transforms into a monster in the movie An American Werewolf in London. **It was one of two popular werewolf films released in 1981.**

• Also released in 1981—but far from humorous— is *The Howling*. A television news anchor (played by Dee Wallace) helps police trap a killer who has been stalking her. Traumatized, she is admitted with her husband to a remote treatment facility. The location turns out to be a werewolf colony. The journalist and her husband both become lycanthropes. In the stunning climax, she transforms into a wolf creature during a newscast, attempting to alert viewers to the reality of werewolves.

- *Teen Wolf* in 1985 marks a return of lycanthropy both to horror-comedy and to a high school–aged central character. It's also a teen romance. Michel J. Fox plays a student who's frustrated in love and less than spectacular on the basketball court—until he discovers lycanthropy runs in his family. His wolf traits make him a whiz on the court and lead to a happy result in his romantic interests, although not the result he'd wanted at first.

- In *Wolf* (1994), the plot is intertwined bizarrely with romance and professional rivalry. Jack Nicholson plays the role of Will Randall, a publishing house editor who apparently hits a wolf while driving. Getting out of his car to investigate, he is bitten. The editor gradually turns into a wolf, as do others of the cast when bitten in turn. In *Wolf*, as in many other werewolf movies, a silver object is a significant element in the story. A paranormalist gives Randall a silver charm to relieve, if not cure, his lycanthropy.

- Cartoon writers have adapted werewolves into TV and movie animations. *Alvin and the Chipmunks Meet the Wolfman* came out in 2000. It is part of a package of animated movies that feature famous monsters interacting with popular cartoon characters.

- A 2010 made-for-television movie, *The Boy Who Cried Werewolf*, is entirely different from the 1973 film of the same name. Here, family members inherit a castle in Romania. The daughter, played by Victoria Justice, accidentally steps on a vial of a mysterious chemical that makes her a werewolf. Her brother (Chase Ellison) discovers her transformation and becomes a werewolf himself.

Werewolves have been included in casts of television series for half a century. They include the science fiction serial *Doctor Who* (1963–present) and *Dark Shadows*, a gothic soap opera that aired on American television from 1966 to 1971. The 1985 horror-comedy *Teen Wolf* spawned an MTV series of the same name that premiered in 2011. Like the movie, the series is centered on a high school student (played by Tyler Posey) whose life is complicated by his werewolf persona. Unlike the film, it includes other shape-shifting characters in the cast.

THE RETURN OF LARRY TALBOT

The character of Larry (Lawrence) Talbot, the tragic human-monster in the 1941 landmark film *The Wolf Man*, was written into numerous werewolf scripts later on. Probably his most notable reprise was in *The Wolfman*, released in 2010. It is a product of Universal Pictures, formerly Universal Studios, which had also produced the classic film.

While set earlier in time than the original film, *The Wolfman* plot has marked similarities to its predecessor. They include the

In the 2010 film The Wolfman, *actor Benicio del Toro revived the role of tragic lycanthrope Larry Talbot, originally portrayed by Lon Chaney Jr.*

central characters—Talbot, his father, and Gwen Conliffe. But in the new version, Lawrence's brother is killed by a monster in a forest, not in an accident. Gwen was his brother's fiancée. And Lawrence's father, played by Anthony Hopkins, turns out to be a werewolf himself.

FRIENDLY LYCANTHROPES

In the early years of the werewolf phenomenon in films and novels, most werewolf characters were presented as frightful monsters. Audiences were touched, however, by their tragic plight as humans who couldn't help what was happening to them.

More recently, many authors and screenwriters have markedly altered the popular perception of lyanthropes. Their characters are still fearsome when in wolf form, but by and large they lead innocent, helpful lives. Some manage to focus their savage energies against villains—which makes them heroes.

A case in point is Luke Garroway (Lucian Graymark), one of the protagonists in Cassandra Clare's *The Mortal Instruments* series of juvenile fantasy novels, which began publication in 2007. The cast is a Who's Who of shape-shifting types: "shadowhunter" warriors, vampires, faeries, fallen angels, warlocks, witches, and werewolves. Throughout the series, Luke is a faithful adult ally of the teenage central character, Clary Fray. Clary does not realize until a crisis comes that he is the leader of a werewolf pack. The werewolves fight on the side of Clary and her shadowhunter friends. Luke is a long-time friend of her mother's, whom he eventually marries.

Benicio del Toro portrays Talbot in the modern remake. The Puerto Rican actor was riveted to the early horror films as a child and was influenced especially by the work of Lon Chaney Jr.

Critics gave *The Wolfman* mixed evaluations, and its box office earnings were modest. Still, it earned an Oscar for best makeup.

WEREWOLF STARS OF THE TWENTY-FIRST CENTURY

Werewolves today are as popular as ever in fantasy literature and films. With the exception of Lawrence Talbot in *The Wolfman* (2010), though, their roles have become secondary. By and large, fictional werewolves today take their place among complex casts of shape-shifting characters.

In the *Twilight* film series, based on the novels of Stephenie Meyer, Jacob Black (portrayed by Taylor Lautner) is the leading werewolf. He is a protector and love interest of Bella Swan, heroine of the series.

Luke Garroway is the champion werewolf in *The Mortal Instruments* series of novels by Cassandra Clare. The first book was made into a 2013 movie, *The Mortal Instruments: City of Bones*. Actor Aidan Turner portrayed Garroway.

In the enormously popular *Harry Potter* novels and films, Remus Lupin, Harry's teacher and friend, is revealed to be a werewolf. Lupin is portrayed in the movies by David Thewlis and James Utechin.

Taylor Lautner plays the role of Jacob Black, a heroic werewolf/shape-shifter in the Twilight *film series. This scene is from the movie* **The Twilight Saga: New Moon.**

The *Underworld* series of action-horror films (2003–present) features werewolves and vampires as immortal characters. The *True Blood* TV series likewise includes werewolves in the cast. It is based on Charlaine Harris's *The Southern Vampire Mysteries*, a series of fantasy novels.

Some of the werewolves in modern fiction are referred to as "lycans" (short for "lycanthropes"). They are different from traditional werewolves in that they can transform themselves at will, not just at the full moon. This ability gives them much greater freedom of action as heroes and villains. They also take advantage of what their writer-creators describe as mind-enhancing qualities of lycanthropy.

CHAPTER 4

A VIRAL PHENOMENON

There was nothing at all scary about "Werewolves of London," a rollicking Top 40 hit song in 1978. It made light of the 1935 and 1941 films. Listeners were amused by the howling of singer Warren Zevon in the refrain. It had a lively beat—fun to dance to.

The song is just one example of the growing legacy of the werewolf as an entertainment theme. Today's werewolves include men, women, and children. They're often depicted as almost ordinary. In the 1960s television sitcom *The Munsters*, the child Eddie Munster, played by Butch Patrick, was a werewolf. He resembled other elementary school children except for his deeply pointed hairline at the forehead and his pointed ears.

Some latter-day werewolves, meantime, are superheroes. Wolf-human creatures appear in comic books and video games.

WEREWOLVES IN MUSIC, WRITING, COMICS, AND GAMES

Five years after Zevon's "Werewolves of London" made the rock music charts, *Michael Jackson's Thriller* video riveted Jackson's millions of fans. It cast the werewolf in a fresh light as a fantasy creature. In the wildly popular 1983 video for his hit song, Jackson portrayed a young man who transforms into

Michael Jackson in **Michael Jackson's Thriller** *music video, produced to accompany his hit song by the same title. Jackson was depicted as a werecat.*

a werecat. Jackson reportedly got the idea from the 1981 film *An American Werewolf in London*.

Other musicians have alluded to werewolf characters in some of their songs. They range from the heavy metal group Iced Earth to the indie rock band Florence and the Machine.

Best-selling fantasy authors such as J. K. Rowling (the *Harry Potter* series), Cassandra Clare, and Stephenie Meyer have incorporated werewolf characters in their plots. Their werewolves often appear in a likeable vein. Among the many other modern writers who have created werewolf characters are Vicki Lewis Thompson, Cassie Alexander, Whitley Strieber, Amanda Carlson, and Cynthia Garner. Werewolf comic book serials have been produced by Dell, Marvel, Moonstone, and other comics publishers since the 1960s.

The phenomenal popularity of fantasy series such as Stephenie Meyer's *Twilight* has spawned a wave of werewolf fan fiction on the Internet. Young people join werewolf clubs and interact in different roles within wolf forums ("packs"). A number of online game sites feature werewolf categories. There are also werewolf board games.

"AM I A WEREWOLF?"

People's fascination with werewolves in modern films and fiction has given rise to a peculiar disorder. It's known as clinical lycanthropy, the psychological condition of young people and adults fantasizing that they are werewolves. Reported incidents

MODERN WEREWOLF SCARES

Thanks no doubt to the popularity of werewolves in pop culture, werewolves "live" in many communities today. For example, some residents of Marshall, Texas, talk of the "man wolf" or "dog man" of Stagecoach Road. Legend holds that the creature has killed countless chickens, cows, and sheep—as well as humans. It reportedly is more than 6 feet (1.8 meters) tall when standing upright. It is said to be hairy and has yellowish eyes, long teeth, and the snout of a wolf.

The "Bray Road Beast" has been reported numerous times around Elkhorn, Wisconsin, since 1936 (the year after *Werewolf of London* was released). Newspaper reports have labeled it a of the disorder have increased in recent decades as the werewolf theme has become ever more popular in multiple media.

Clinical lycanthropes are people who believe they can change into animals, or have done so in the past. Some patients act like animals—growling or crawling on all fours, for example. Some insist they "feel" like an animal. Symptoms include unnatural behavior: howling; eating the things that animals eat, such as hay; insisting on living outdoors; and so forth. Some patients are convinced they have fangs or claws.

Not all clinical lycanthropes believe themselves to be werewolves. Most, in fact, perceive themselves as other species: dogs, foxes, cats, horses, tigers, birds, frogs, bees, and others.

Many psychologists believe clinical lycanthropy in a patient is part of a broader, more common disorder such as schizophrenia or clinical depression. The condition may be rooted partly in cultural traditions. Interestingly, the word "lycanthropy" has been compared to "melancholy." Melancholy is a common state of mild depression.

An obsession with the werewolf concept can be disturbing and suggest a person's dark side. It's noteworthy that Adolf Hitler was fascinated by wolves and werewolves. That no doubt stemmed from the meaning of his name. "Adolf" derives from the ancient German "Adalwolf"—"Noble Wolf." Early in his secretive rise to political power, he used the codename "Herr Wolf." Members of the Hitler Youth corps were taught that they, like wolves, must learn to act with insensitive cruelty and to ignore pain. One of his military bunkers in World War II was dubbed "Wolfsschanze" ("Wolf's Lair"). German U-boats prowled the Atlantic in squadrons called wolfpacks. He and his generals conceived a war plan called Operation Werwolf, sending guerrilla forces to operate behind enemy lines. The name came from a German historical novel by Hermann Lons titled *Der Wehrwolf*.

Some psychologists believe Hitler showed clinical lycanthropic symptoms. In his personal life, he named his German shepherd "Wolf." It was reported that when relaxing, he often whistled the *Three Little Pigs* cartoon theme song, "Who's Afraid of the Big Bad Wolf?"

OCTOBER MADNESS

Every October, grotesquely costumed "werewolves" leap from the shadows to terrify paying visitors to haunted houses, haunted corn mazes, haunted woods, and haunted cemeteries at Halloween time. Some of the local actors use store-bought masks, hair suits, and plastic fangs. Others go into careful detail to make themselves appear as realistic as possible.

Costumes and makeup techniques present many of today's werewolves of screen and stage as ferocious animal figures. But interestingly, a lot of the werewolves people encounter along haunted trails and at costume parties still look strikingly like Lon Chaney Jr. in *The Wolf Man*, circa 1941. His classic movie werewolf lives on.

FILMOGRAPHY

Werewolf of London (1935)
Director: Stuart Walker
Actors: Henry Hull and
Warner Oland

The Wolf Man (1941)
Director: George Waggner
Actors: Lon Chaney Jr. and
Claude Rains

The Mad Monster (1942)
Director: Sam Newfield
Actors: Johnny Downs and
George Zucco

**Frankenstein Meets the
Wolf Man** (1943)
Director: Roy William Neill
Actors: Lon Chaney Jr. and Bela
Lugosi

**I Was a Teenage
Werewolf** (1957)
Director: Gene Fowler Jr.
Actors: Michael Landon and Whit
Bissell

Lycanthropus (1962)
Director: Paolo Heusch
Actors: Carl Shell, Barbara Lass,
and Curt Lowens

**The Boy Who Cried
Werewolf** (1973)
Director: Nathan H. Juran
Actors: Kerwin Mathews, Elaine
Devry, and Scott Sealey

The Howling (1981)
Director: Joe Dante
Actors: Dee Wallace and Patrick
Macnee

An American Werewolf in London (1981)
Director: John Landis
Actors: David Naughton, Griffin Dunne, and Jenny Agutter

Teen Wolf (1985)
Director: Rod Daniel
Actors: Michael J. Fox and Lorie Griffin

Wolf (1994)
Director: Mike Nichols
Actors: Jack Nicholson and Michelle Pfeiffer

The Wolfman (2010)
Director: Joe Johnston
Actors: Benicio del Toro and Anthony Hopkins

GLOSSARY

ALLEGE To claim or declare that someone has done something wrong or unlawful without proof.

ALLUDE To hint at or refer to.

ANTIDOTE A drug that can cure or diminish a particular illness.

CLINICAL Causing recognizable signs, as in an illness.

CRYPT A family burial vault.

CULT CLASSIC A film that is admired by a small but devoted fan base.

DEMONIAC Relating to a demon or demons.

DIGITIZED Stored and distributed as electronic media.

FAN FICTION Stories about a popular character written by fans.

FICTIONAL Created by the imagination, not actual.

FOLKLORE The body of legends and customs passed down through generations.

ICON A real or fictitious person with a large, devoted following.

INJECT To force liquid into a body.

LAIR The place where a wild animal lives, such as a den; a hideaway.

MEDIEVAL Referring to the Middle Ages.

MIDDLE AGES Roughly the sixth through fifteenth centuries.

MONASTERY The establishment where monks live and work.

MOORS Open grassland or marsh where few trees or crops grow.

MYTHOLOGY A collection of beliefs about gods and superhumans.

PENTAGRAM An occult symbol in the shape of a five-pointed star.

PROTAGONIST The main character.

REPRISE A repeated role or performance.

SERUM A liquid drug concoction.

SORCERER Wizard.

FOR MORE INFORMATION

Academy of Motion Picture Arts and Sciences

49 Wilshire Boulevard

Beverly Hills, CA 90211

(310) 247-3000

Website: http://www.oscars.org

The academy, sponsor of the Academy Awards (Oscars), maintains a vast film collection and features the Academy Museum, the world's primary film museum.

Academy of Science Fiction Fantasy and Horror Films

334 West 54th Street

Los Angeles, CA 90037

(323) 752-5811

Website: http://www.saturnawards.org

Founded in 1972, the academy sponsors the Saturn Awards honoring professionals involved in genre movies and television productions.

American Film Institute (AFI)

2021 North Western Avenue

Los Angeles, CA 90027-1657

(323) 856-7600

Website: http://www.afi.com

Resources of the American Film Institute include the AFI Catalog of Feature Films. The AFI catalogs all commercially produced American films since 1893.

Motion Picture Association of America, Inc. (MPAA)

1600 I Street NW

Washington, DC 20006-4010

(202) 293-1966

Website: http://www.mpaa.org

The MPAA is "the voice and advocate of the American motion picture, home video and television industries." Its "Where to Watch" web section links to outlets where you can obtain movies and TV shows online for your PC, tablet, or smartphone.

Motion Picture Association–Canada

55 St. Clair Avenue West, Suite 210

Toronto, ON M4V 2Y7

Canada

(416) 961-1888

Website: http://www.mpa-canada.org

The MPA-Canada is the Canadian affiliate of the Motion Picture Association of America.

WEBSITES

Because of the changing nature of Internet links, Rosen Publishing has developed an online list of websites related to the subject of this book. This site is updated regularly. Please use this link to access the list:

http://www.rosenlinks.com/GMM/Were

FOR FURTHER READING

Connolly, Kieron. *World's Worst Monsters & Villains: Scary Creatures of Myth, Folklore, and Fiction*. New York, NY: Scholastic Books, 2012.

Dell, Christopher. *Monsters: A Bestiary of Devils, Demons, Vampires, Werewolves, and Other Magical Creatures*. Rochester, VT: Inner Traditions, 2010.

DK Publishing. *Children's Book of Mythical Beasts and Magical Monsters*. London, UK: DK Children, 2011.

Hardwicke, Catherine. *Twilight Director's Notebook: The Story of How We Made the Movie Based on the Novel by Stephenie Meyer*. New York, NY: Little, Brown Young Readers, 2009.

McCall, Gerrie, and Lisa Regan. *Half Man, Half Monster* (Monsters & Myths). New York, NY: Gareth Stevens Publishing, 2011.

McCall, Gerrie. *Monsters and Villains of the Movies and Literature*. New York, NY: Scholastic Books, 2008.

McCall, Gerrie, and Chris McNab. *Mythical Monsters: Legendary, Fearsome Creatures*. New York, NY: Scholastic Books, 2011.

McNab, Chris. *Mythical Monsters: The Scariest Creatures from Legends, Books, and Movies*. New York, NY: Tangerine Press (Scholastic), 2006.

Regan, Lisa, and Chris McNab. *Urban Myths and Legendary Creatures* (Monsters & Myths). New York, NY: Gareth Stevens Publishing, 2011.

Regan, Lisa. *Vampires, Werewolves & Zombies*. New York, NY: Scholastic Books, 2009.

Renfield, R. K. *Meet the Wolf Man* (Famous Movie Monsters). New York, NY: Rosen Publishing, 2005.

Roza, Greg. *Introducing Frankenstein Meets the Wolfman* (Famous Movie Monsters). New York, NY: Rosen Publishing, 2006.

BIBLIOGRAPHY

Beaugrand, Henry. "The Werwolves." Originally published in 1898, reprinted at the Gaslight website. Retrieved October 2014 (http://gaslight.mtroyal.ca/werwolvs.htm).

Delahoyde, Michael A. "The Wolf Man (1941)." English 338 course resources, Washington State University. Retrieved October 2014 (http://public.wsu.edu/~delahoyd/wolfman41.html).

Gilchrist, Todd. "Rick Baker Says He's Still Stinging About 'The Wolfman.'" *The Playlist* blog, September 26, 2011. Retrieved October 2014 (http://blogs.indiewire.com/theplaylist/rick_baker_hes_still_stinging_about_the_wolfman_says_despite_oscar_win_cgi).

Horror Film History. "Horror Movies of the 1940s." Retrieved November 2014 (www.horrorfilmhistory.com/index.php?pageID=1940s).

Jones, Jason. "The Wolf Man (1941)." Classic-Horror.com. Retrieved October 2014 (http://classic-horror.com/reviews/wolf_man_1941).

Nickell, Joe. *Tracking the Man-Beasts: Sasquatch, Vampires, Zombies, and More*. Amherst, NY: Prometheus Books, 2011.

Phipps, Keith, and Noel Murray. "A Guide to the Universal Studios Monster Movies, 1923–1955." *A.V. Club*, October 25, 2012. Retrieved November 2014 (www.avclub.com/article/a-guide-to-the-universal-studios-monster-movies-19-87883).

Random Facts. "72 Random Facts About . . . Adolf Hitler." Retrieved November 2014 (http://facts.randomhistory.com/hitler-facts.html).

Steiger, Brad. *The Werewolf Book: The Encyclopedia of Shape-Shifting Beings*. 2nd ed. Canton, MI: Visible Ink Press, 2012.

Turner Classic Movies database. "The Wolf Man (1941)." Retrieved October 2014 (www.tcm.com/tcmdb/title/96098/The-Wolf-Man).

YouTube. "100 Years of Werewolf Movies, Part 1." Retrieved October 2014 (www.youtube.com/watch?v=J-pgJxgoAf8).

Zevon, Warren. "Werewolves of London." YouTube video. Retrieved August 2014 (www.youtube.com/watch?v=nhSc8qVMjKM).

INDEX

ABOUT THE AUTHOR

Daniel E. Harmon has written more than ninety books on topics including entertainment, history, careers, regional and international studies, and health science. His biographies include *Cassandra Clare* (2015). He has contributed thousands of articles to national and regional periodicals and is a veteran magazine and newsletter editor. He also writes historical crime short stories. Harmon lives in Spartanburg, South Carolina.

PHOTO CREDITS

Cover © AF archive/Alamy; p. 5 © Mary Evans Picture Library/Alamy; p. 7 © Chronicle/Alamy; p. 10 Brian North/Dorling Kindersley/Getty Images; p. 13 Universal Images Group/Getty Images; pp. 15, 16, 19, 22, 26, 35 courtesy Everett Collection; p. 27 © Pictorial Press Ltd/Alamy; p. 30 Frank Connor/© Universal Pictures/courtesy Everett Collection; p. 33 Photofest; pp. 40–41 Andrey_Kuzmin/Shutterstock.com; interior pages banners and backgrounds Nik Merkulov/Shutterstock.com, Apostrophe/Shutterstock.com.

Designer: Brian Garvey; Editor: Kathy Kuhtz Campbell